So very...

Harrogate

[with a bit of Knaresborough and Starbeck too]

Photography by Richard Jemison & Nigel Whitfield
Design and research by Wendy Jemison

Richard Jemison: Teesside born; Northallerton based; freelance photographer

Nigel Whitfield: Hexham born; Great Langton based; freelance photographer

So Very Harrogate (With a Bit of Knaresborough
and Starbeck Too)

By Richard Jemison & Nigel Whitfield
Designed by Wendy Jemison
Published by Sovery Books
Printed by Colour It In Ltd., Harrogate

First published in 2014
ISBN: 978-0-9928613-0-8

A Foreword
by Lord Crathorne KCVO

"Anyone who has visited Harrogate and sampled its charms will greatly enjoy this book. It captures the essence of the town and its surrounding area in a collection of photographs which are both technically advanced and creatively absorbing, many revealing unexpected views of the familiar. I have had the pleasure of knowing and admiring Richard and Nigel's work for some years. When we meet we always have interesting discussions about photography."

James Crathorne, March 2014

Lord Crathorne is Lord-Lieutenant of North Yorkshire. He is also the co-photographer of 'Parliament in Pictures' published by Thames and Hudson, and is Secretary to the All-Party Photography group at Westminster.

1. First impressions...

"Harrogate is the queerest place with the strangest people in it,
leading the oddest lives of dancing, newspaper reading and dining."

Charles Dickens, 1858

"Built by Baggalley and Bristowe of London at a cost of £120 000, the Baths were formally opened in 1897.

In addition to the Turkish Baths, more than a dozen other types of bath, douche or treatment were available, together with a full complement of consulting doctors.

A Turkish bath cost three shillings and a massage two shillings. The Baths' Moorish design with great Islamic arches and screens, its walls of vibrant glazed brickwork, the arabesque painted ceilings and terrazzo floors (imported from Italy) all add to its historic fantasy qualities."

Treatments 1898

Intestinal Lavage Treatment: the two-way continuous irrigation system was used in cases of colitis, constipation and for intestinal problems.

The Peat Baths: this treatment was much prescribed. Needle Baths were used not only for removing peat, but also acted as a skin tonic. The mineral for these baths, containing organic acids and iron, was obtained from the Yorkshire Moors. The baths were used to treat rheumatism, sciatica, circulation, back and pelvic disorders.

2. The Turkish Baths

BOROUGH OF HARROGATE

CORONATION
OF
HER GRACIOUS MAJESTY
QUEEN ELIZABETH II.

Commemorative Planting

of 200

Flowering Cherry Trees

(Cerasus Serrulata Kanzan)

On the York Place Stray on

Saturday, 28th February, 1953,

at 2-30 p.m.

The MAYOR and MAYORESS (Councillor and Mrs. A. V. Milton), School Children and Members of Youth Organisations will personally plant trees following a Dedication Ceremony conducted by the Mayor's Chaplain, Revd. R. H. Baines, M.A.

Grow for Winter
as well as Summer

Vegetables for you and your family every week of the year. Never a week without food from your garden or allotment. Not only fresh peas and lettuce in June - new potatoes in July, but all the health-giving vegetables in WINTER - when supplies are scarce... SAVOYS, SPROUTS, KALE, SPROUTING BROCCOLI, ONIONS, LEEKS, CARROTS, PARSNIPS and BEET

Vegetables all the year round
if you
DIG WELL
AND CROP WISELY

1940s

now...

5. *Victorian* to Contemporary via **Brutalism**

Victorian architecture is characterised by massive construction and elaborate ornamentation, with features such as bay windows, cornices, dormers, dentils, patterned bricks and stained glass.

Brutalist architecture flourished from the 1950s to the mid-1970s. Examples are typically very linear, fortress-like and blockish, often with a predominance of architectural concrete, left unfinished or roughly- finished after pouring and left exposed visually [from the French, 'Béton brut'].

Contemporary architecture is an evolution of modern architecture. Connecting indoor and outdoor spaces, expansive windows and green building are often strong components of the contemporary style.

Valley Gardens were originally developed as an attractive walk for visitors to the Spa town, part of their health regime between taking the waters, as well as a means of access to the mineral springs of Bogs Field. The waterside walk, with flowers and trees, became a favourite place for promenading and socialising. In the early 20th century the gardens were an enormously popular location, with crowds gathering around the tea room, boating lake and bandstand.

The Sun Pavilion and Colonnades were opened in 1933 as an added attraction and facility for the spa, intended as the first phase of a covered way linking the Pump Room and Royal Bath Hospital.

Over the years visitors to the mineral springs may have declined, but the horticultural reputation of the Gardens continues to grow.

6. Valley Gardens, Colonnades

7. Mother Shipton's Cave

Mother Shipton was a Yorkshire 'witch', born in a cave in 1488, who prophesied future events. She predicted the invention of iron ships, the Great Fire of London, the defeat of the Spanish Armada, even the end of the world!

Millions have visited Mother Shipton's cave and seen the amazing powers of the nearby ancient Petrifying Well, thought to be the only one of its kind in England. At the time of Mother Shipton, local townsfolk believed the well to be magic, having seen twigs, leaves, perhaps dead birds, turned to stone in its falling waters. They feared superstitiously that, if they touched the waters, they too would be turned to stone!

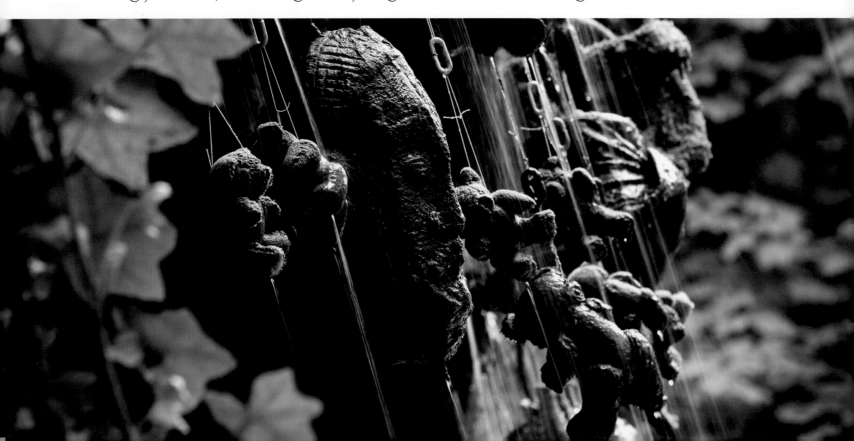

To commemorate the discovery of the medicinal waters of Harrogate

PUMP  ROOM,

OLD
SULPHUR WELL, HARROGATE.

The celebrated Strong Sulphur Water, which springs on the premises, is supplied to drinkers in its natural state, direct from the well, as is the Mild Sulphur which also springs on the premises, and are heated by Mr. R. H. Davis's Therma, the best known apparatus for heating mineral waters.

The other waters supplied at the Room, brought direct from the Bogs field, are the Magnesia, the Alexandra or strong Saline Chalybeate, and the pure Chalybeate, or carbonate of iron water.

TERMS FOR DRINKING THE WATERS.

	Strong Sulphur.	Mild Sulphur.	Magnesia·
Per Day	3d.	3d.	3d.
Per Week	1s. 6.	1s. 6d.	1s 0d.

The Strong Sulphur and Magnesia Waters, or the Strong Sulphur and Mild Sulphur Waters when taken together, are charged at the rate of 4d. per day or 2s. per week.

Alexandra Chalybeate.	Pure Chalybeate.
Per Day 4d.	Per Day 4d.
Per Week 2s.	Per Week 2s.

Children under twelve half-price.

BOTTLING DEPARTMENT.

The Waters are carefully bottled direct from the springs, in special bottles, (impressed with the Trade Mark), by experienced bottlers, and are sent to all parts, at the following prices, bottles and hampers included :—

Strong Sulphur, Old Well	24 oz. bottles	per doz	6s. 0d.
Do. Do.	12 oz. ,,	,,	4s. 6d.
Mild Sulphur	24 oz. ,,	,,	6s. 0d.
Do.	12 oz. ,,	,,	4s. 6d.
Magnesia	24 oz. ,,	,,	6s. 0d.
Do.	12 oz. ,,	,,	4s. 6d.
Alexadra Chalybeate	4 oz. ,,	,,	5s. 0d.
Pure Chalybeate	4 oz. ,,	,,	5s. 0d.

Terms, Cash with Order.

An allowance of 1s. 6d. per dozen for the 24oz. bottles is made for returned empties, and 1s. per dozen for the 12 oz. bottles, if returned free.

P.O. ORDERS TO

ILLIAM HIGGS, LESSEE.

9. The Four Seasons

Where is Mrs Christie?

On the 3rd December 1926 Agatha Christie kissed her sleeping daughter goodbye and walked out of her family home to vanish for eleven days. Her disappearance caused ripples of speculation across the world, as a massive manhunt failed to locate the famous author.

Earlier that day Archie, Agatha's husband, had revealed that he wished to divorce her, and then left to spend the weekend with his mistress. Agatha drove off into the night, later abandoning her car. She left a single clue, a letter, saying she was going to visit Yorkshire.

Agatha registered into the Swan Hydropathic Hotel [now Old Swan Hotel], in Harrogate. It was ten days later before she was identified.

Agatha Christie never offered an explanation for her disappearance, though several theories have been suggested. These range from depression, amnesia, 'psychogenic fugue', to theories that the whole affair was a planned publicity stunt or even an attempt to embarrass or frame her errant husband. The couple divorced two years later, in 1928.

10. The Old Swan Hotel

First staged in 1966, the Great Knaresborough Bed Race is something different, part fancy dress pageant and part gruelling time trial over a 2.4 mile course, ending with a swim through the icy waters of the River Nidd.

Each team, made up of six runners and one passenger, must provide a bed, decorated in the theme for the year [not exceeding 2 metres in width, 4 metres in length and 3 metres in height, with a built in buoyancy aid], an audible air horn or hooter, along with a helmet and life jacket for the passenger.

13. Christmas in Harrogate

Harrogate Spring Water

... boasts an excellent mineral balance. The water is naturally very low in sodium, but rich in magnesium and calcium and is virtually absent of nitrates. Its high bicarbonate levels give the water its delicate sweet taste.

Crimplene

In the 1950s, ICI Fibres Laboratory, based in Crimple Valley, developed a revolutionary new fabric. Crimplene was made of a thick polyester yarn. The fabric was heavy, crease resistant and kept its shape, the ultimate in wash and wear.

Farrah's Original Harrogate Toffee

John Farrah established Farrah's in 1840. The Original Harrogate Toffee was designed to clear the palate of the putrid taste of Harrogate's Sulphur Water, which was famous for its healing properties in the 19th century.

15. The Victoria Shopping Centre

16. Harlow Carr in Summer

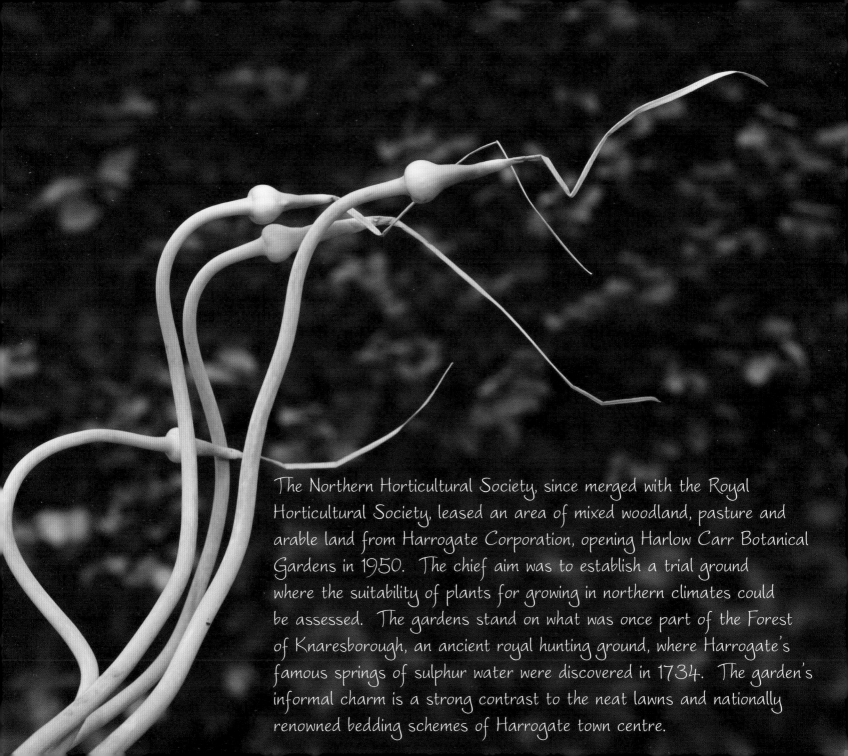

The Northern Horticultural Society, since merged with the Royal Horticultural Society, leased an area of mixed woodland, pasture and arable land from Harrogate Corporation, opening Harlow Carr Botanical Gardens in 1950. The chief aim was to establish a trial ground where the suitability of plants for growing in northern climates could be assessed. The gardens stand on what was once part of the Forest of Knaresborough, an ancient royal hunting ground, where Harrogate's famous springs of sulphur water were discovered in 1734. The garden's informal charm is a strong contrast to the neat lawns and nationally renowned bedding schemes of Harrogate town centre.

17. Harlow Carr in Winter

It is believed that a Saxon fortification existed on the site of the current castle, known at the time as Chednaresburg. The first mention of the castle was in 1129, when expenditure of eleven pounds was recorded as being spent on the royal stronghold by its custodian Eustice Fitz-John.

One of the castle's more notorious associations was in 1170, when its knight, Hugh de Morville, sought refuge within its walls, along with the other murderers of Archbishop Thomas Beckett in Canterbury Cathedral.

In 1205 King John took over control and spent £1 290 on improvements to the castle, which was an important northern fortress and offered good hunting in the surrounding medieval forest. Over the years, successive owners continued to invest and make improvements to the castle as it moved in and out of royal ownership. Sometimes this ownership transferred peacefully, sometimes as a result of besiegement.

In 1642, at the beginning of the Civil War, the castle was in Royalist ownership. Within two years most of Yorkshire had succumbed to the Parliamentarians, on 20th December 1644, following a siege lasting several weeks, Knaresborough Castle finally surrendered to the opposing forces.

Since the early 1900s the ruins of Knaresborough Castle have been used as a public park.

18. Knaresborough Castle

The Majestic's gentlemen's lavatory hall hit national news in 1995. When faced with the need for additional lavatory facilities for ladies, the decision was made to divide the gentlemen's lavatory. The spacious hall, with its floor of polished marble, mahogany panelling, brass fittings, settees and potted palms, was provided with a partition. Outrage followed, even with letters to the Times! Eventually they relented, the hall was restored to its Victorian splendour and separate accommodation provided elsewhere for the ladies. A celebration party was held in the gentlemen's hall, with ladies invited – solely for this occasion!

PRICE : SIXPENCE

HARROGATE

SHOPPING WEEK

May 19·26

"Buy it in Harrogate"

20. Buy it in Harrogate

The 30 acre park and large picturesque garden, formerly known as Plompton Rocks, was formed in the 1760s by creating a lake at the foot of an extensive range of weathered and contorted grit stone outcrops.

The artist J.M.W. Turner painted two oil paintings of Plumpton Rocks following his first visit to Yorkshire in 1797. Turner was commissioned by Edward Lascelles, 1st Earl of Harewood, who owned the estate of Plumpton Rocks at that time.

These were Turner's first commissioned landscapes in oils and he charged the Earl a little more than £32 for the pair. Within a few years the artist was so successful, he could charge twenty times that amount.

22. Plumpton Rocks

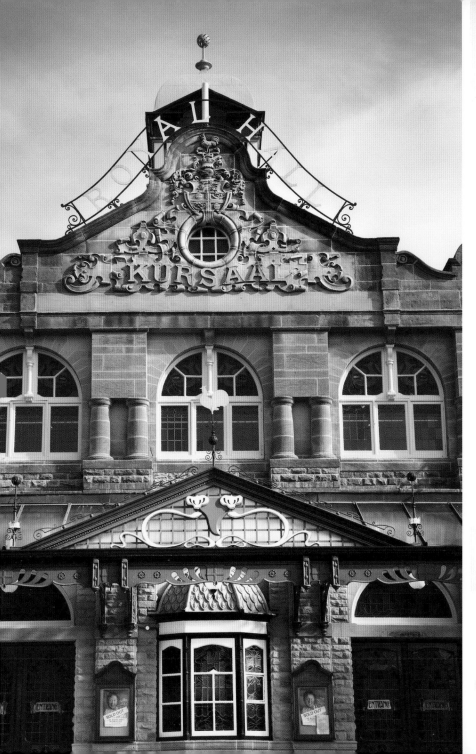

THE KURSAAL
and ROYAL SPA,
HARROGATE

MANAGER .... } For the...... { MR. H. J. DACRE.
MUSICAL DIRECTOR } Corporation. { MR. C. L. NAYLOR, M.A., Mus. Bac. (Cantab)

Grand
Opening Concert,
Wednesday, May 27th, 1903.

Opening Ceremony
AT 7-45 BY
SIR HUBERT PARRY, BART.,
D.C.L., MUS. DOC.
(Director of the Royal College of Music).
FOLLOWED BY
A Grand Ballad and
Orchestral Concert.

Artistes :—
MISS MARIE HALL,
SOLO VIOLINIST.
(Mr. HENRY BIRD, of London, Accompanist)

Miss EMILY DAVIES, Soprano: AND THE GRAND
Mr. GREGORY HAST, Tenor: Municipal Orchestra
Mr. GRIFFITH PERCY, Bass: of 50 Performers.
                          Under the direction of
                  Mr. C. L. NAYLOR, M.A., Mus. Bac. (Cantab)

SIR HUBERT PARRY, Bart., will conduct the Orchestra
in one of his own compositions.

The Kursaal has been perfumed
by Mr. A. Atkinson, Chemist,
Parliament St., with Potter &
Moore's celebrated Mitcham
Lavender Water.

S. R. LUPTON, PRINTER, HARROGATE.

Facsimile of the cover of the Programme of the First Concert.

23.
The Royal Hall

Knaresborough Viaduct was engineered by Thomas Grainger to carry Victorian rail traffic over the River Nidd. The viaduct's construction was not straight forward however. On the 11th of March 1848, shortly before completion, it collapsed, sending tons of rubble crashing down the gorge, completely damming the river below.

When the Knaresborough-York line opened in October 1848, with the viaduct still in ruins, trains had to terminate at a temporary station about a mile from the town centre.

The tunnel at Knaresborough was finished by August 1849 and the contract to rebuild the viaduct re-let to different contractors. This did not please the original contractors who fenced off the works to prevent anyone taking possession. They also threw the fallen rubble back into the river as fast as the new contractors' men brought it out.

Eventually rebuilt by Duckett and Stead, the final keystone of the 90ft high and 338ft long viaduct was laid on the 30th of August 1850.

24. Knaresborough Viaduct

Built just before the turn of the century, Harrogate Theatre opened on the 11th of January 1900 with a charity gala in aid of British soldiers fighting in the Boer War. This was followed two days later by Mr J. Tully's pantomime, 'Dick Whittington'.

Originally known as 'The Grand Opera House', the theatre was designed by architect, Frank Tugwell. The theatre incorporated many of the latest safety features, a fire-proof curtain which could be lowered between the stage and the auditorium, fire extinguishers, a sprinkler system and stairs and corridors constructed of stone.

The theatre was lavishly decorated with gilded plasterwork mouldings and boasted hot and cold running water in the dressing rooms, as well as electric lighting.

Over the last one hundred years or so, many famous names of stage and screen have trodden the boards at Harrogate Theatre; Trevor Howard, Charlie Chaplin, Sarah Bernhardt, Arnold Ridley, Martin Shaw and Ben Kingsley to name but a few.

25. Harrogate Theatre

26. The Art of the Theatre

The carved frieze in the foyer of Harrogate Theatre was not part of the original décor, thought to have been added shortly before 1911. The magnificent seventy-foot frieze, sculpted by Frances Darlington, comprises eleven richly modelled plaster panels depicting themes from drama and literature and the development of arts through the ages. Frances Darlington [880-1939], was the daughter of a Harrogate solicitor. She studied sculpture in London at the progressive Slade School of Art and then at the School of Art and Design in South Kensington.

Primula Auricula
Spr...

Primula Auricula
Strawberry Fields

Primula Auricula
Elsie May

Primula Auricula
...ing

Primula Auricula
Sunny Brow

Primula Auricula
Blush Baby

Primula Auricula
Knights

Primula Auricula
Lilac Domino

Primula Auricula
Limelight

Primula Auricula
Sharmans Cross

27. Great Yorkshire Showground

The Great Yorkshire Show was born in October 1837 when a group of leading agriculturalists, led by the third Earl Spencer, met at the Black Swan Hotel in Coney Street, York to discuss the future of the farming industry. The show was originally a peripatetic event, travelling to different locations across Yorkshire. Its current permanent site in Harrogate was purchased in 1950 for a price of £16 500. The first recorded attendance was 6 044 in 1842, whilst the highest number to date was recorded in 2006, when a staggering 135 111 visitors paid to attend the annual show.

28. Our Lady of the Crag

High up in the crag face above Knaresborough's River Nidd stands a small building hewn into the rock; a 15th Century carving of a Knight keeping watch at its door. In 1408 the Chapel of Our Lady of The Crag was excavated as a wayside shrine by the stonemason, John the Mason. The story goes that the stonemason's son was almost killed by a rock fall in the quarry and that he prayed fervently to the Virgin Mary to save him. When his son emerged from the rubble, miraculously unscathed, John built the chapel in thanksgiving.

Permission for the shrine was granted in a royal charter from King Henry IV. The Chapel shows the work of the master craftsman, with a carved altar, vaulted ceiling, roof bosses and gargoyles, looking every bit like an erected building, but with a special quality of being created from the crag itself.

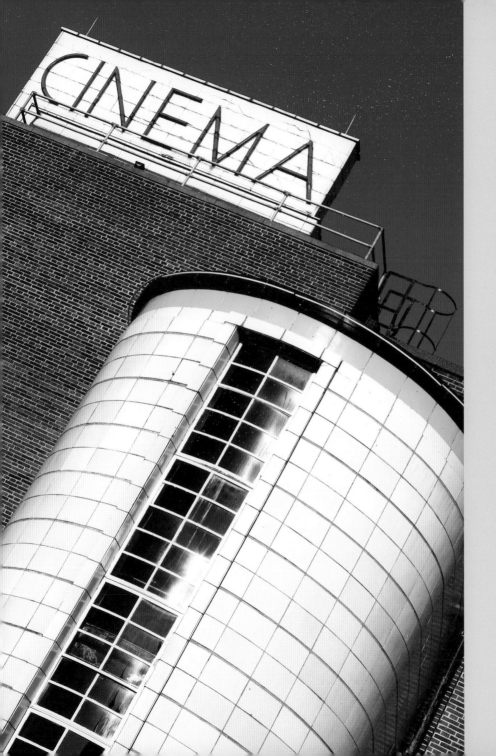

& ART DECO

Like the majority of Odeon cinemas, Harrogate's Odeon was built in the 'Streamlined Moderne' style. With very few exceptions, whilst certain design elements and overall schemes were repeated, each cinema was unique. The Harrogate Odeon, completed in 1936, was designed by Harry Weedon and W. Calder Robson.

A dominant feature of the Odeon's design is its central brown-brick tower, with a projecting, taller 'fin' clad in biscuit-coloured faience tiles. At the top of the fin 'cinema' is spelt out in slender, sans-serif lettering.

Inside the auditorium seating was originally divided into stalls and balcony seating, with 1 647 seats in total.

The building, still a working cinema, was awarded Grade-II listed status in 1988.

30. Night...

...life

31. Tour de Harrogate

So very... taking photographs!

Photography involves decisions about composition and technique. Today's digital cameras generally deal well with most technical challenges, however there are times when they get it wrong. It's important therefore to recognise those times when your own judgement should override that of the camera.

A case in point is the Art Nouveau image [No. 29]. It was getting dark; the window was back-lit. I could have gone back to the car for my tripod, but it was cold and it had been a long day! Most cameras would suggest using a flash to light the shot, but that would not capture the effect of the backlighting passing through the glass. Ideally I would have balanced the light from the front and the back with a 'healthy' f8 aperture at 100 ISO, giving a very long exposure. Unfortunately this would have made it impossible to hand-hold the camera without getting the dreaded 'camera shake'. So, ignoring what the camera suggested, I did the following:

1. increased the ISO to 800, knowing that my camera can deal with any unpleasant side effects concerning noise;

2. used 'RAW' files and deliberately underexposed, corrected for during conversion to TIFF format;

3. shot at f5.6 rather than f8 since I did not require the extra depth of field gained from a smaller aperture.

Combining the above allowed me to increase the shutter speed from an impossibly slow 1 second to a 'hand holdable' 1/60th second. So I ended up with an acceptable, if slightly compromised, photo that is sharp despite the lack of a tripod. Saying all that, I could have run back to the car to get my tripod, but thirty years of experience meant that I didn't need to.

I believe that, with a bit of effort, anyone can make the inbuilt technology suit their needs, rather than always letting the camera dictate the end result.

With thanks to the following for providing photographic inspiration and sources of information:

Farrah's of Harrogate

Harlow Carr Gardens

Harrogate Library

Harrogate Spring Water

Harrogate Theatre

Mother Shipton's Cave

North Yorkshire County Council

The Conference Centre

The Majestic Hotel

The Old Swan Hotel

The Royal Hall

The Royal Pump Room

The Turkish Baths

The Yorkshire Showground

Websites:

www.rhs.org.uk/gardens/harlow-carr

www.farrahs.com

www.greatyorkshireshow.co.uk

www.harrogatespringwater.co.uk

www.turkishbathsharrogate.co.uk

www.mothershipton.co.uk

www.modernistbritain.co.uk/post/building

www.friendsofvalleygardens.co.uk

www.bedrace.co.uk

www.plumptonrocks.com

www.harrogatetheatre.co.uk

www.d.lib.rochester.edu/camelot/creator/frances-darlington

www.knaresborough.co.uk/

www.stmarysknaresborough.org/shrine

and thanks to: artists Steve Blaylock (sculpture – Harlow Carr in Winter) and John Hill (sculpture in memory of Starbeck historian Gordon Beer - Tour de Harrogate)

In: 'Nostalgic Starbeck, the text is from 'Dig for Victory Leaflet No. 1', published by the Ministry of Agriculture (circa 1940) and the World War II 'Dig On For Victory' poster (1939-1945) is by the artist Peter Fraser (1888-1950). The latter is a public domain resource available via Wikimedia Commons.

Coming soon to a place near you...

'So Very Harrogate' is the first in a planned series of books that focus on capturing both the familiar and the remarkable visual appeal of our favourite locations.

A selection of photographs from the books will be made freely available to those purchasing, with images downloadable from www.jemisonphotographer.co.uk.

A second book in the series 'So Very Whitby' is already in progress, and promises to be an exciting project, with publication planned for Autumn 2014. Anyone who has ever enjoyed a visit to Whitby will want this book!

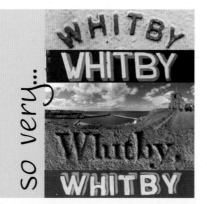

'The images epitomize North Yorkshire with the photographers skilfully capturing the very essence of this beautiful county - its quirks, landscapes and atmospheres' (Rt. Hon. William Hague MP)

NORTH YORKSHIRE ONE NINE NINE
richard jemison, chris firth & nigel whitfield

In 2004 photographer Richard Jemison and writer Chris Firth embarked on a series of books combining innovative photography and powerful poetry. The highly acclaimed 'Whitby One Nine Nine', now out of print, was the first in the series. For their second book, Richard and Chris were joined by photographer Nigel Whitfield. 'North Yorkshire One Nine Nine', was awarded the prestigious title 'Yorkshire Non-Fiction Book of the Year 2007'. It was followed by Teesway One Nine Nine, an inspiring illustration of the River Tees from its source at Cross Fell to its mouth at the North Sea.

NORTH YORKSHIRE ONE NINE NINE
Richard Jemison, Chris Firth & Nigel Whitfield
Shutter Books 2006, ISBN 978-0-9551307-3-1

TEESWAY ONE NINE NINE
Richard Jemison, Chris Firth & Nigel Whitfield
Shutter Books 2007, ISBN 978-0-9551307-5-5